D1742292

Website Copywriting:

The 7 Essential Pages for
Online Business Success

Danny Iny

Jim Hopkinson

Questions

Questions can be sent to support@mirasee.com.

Dedicated to everyone that is putting themselves out there with a message that needs to be heard.

You're an inspiration to others and the team at Mirasee is here to support you.

Thank you!

Website Copywriting Extras

Want a summary of key takeaways from your Kindle book and access to our companion course at a preferential price?

Free PDF Resource Guide
Get your website up and running with minimal effort – no matter what type of business you have.

- Visual examples of website best practices
- Chapter summaries and key points
- Adaptable to suit any website

Online Video Companion Course – 50% OFF coupon
Are you a visual learner? You'll love our video based companion course.

- 60+ minutes of video instruction
- Live walkthroughs of featured sites
- Entertaining and educational

Get your free guide and course coupon:
http://mrse.co/copywriting-extras

Website Links and Further Reading Available Online

In a book about websites, there are going to be
a lot of links.

For your ease of reading, all links to website urls and
further reading referenced in this book have been
neatly organized by chapter, in order of appearance,
on our website:

http://mrse.co/copywriting-links

Enjoy!

Contents

Introduction

Imagine what it was like being a titan of industry at the turn of the century.

John D. Rockefeller was the co-founder of Standard Oil Company, which at one point controlled 90% of all oil in the United States, making him the richest man in the world and the first American billionaire. Andrew Carnegie had business interests in railroad and oil, then built the Carnegie Steel Corporation into the largest steel manufacturing company in the world.

Over in Detroit, Henry Ford built cars that anyone could afford — at one point half of all cars in America were Model T Fords — making him one of the richest people in the world as well.

These titans had something in common. As they

established their dominant position in the market, it was difficult for competitors to challenge them. If you thought you could build a better business in the steel or auto industry, you were welcome to try… as long as you had your own oil rig, steel plant, or assembly line. This high barrier to entry helped each titan accumulate substantial wealth.

Now let's look at roughly the next 100 years, from the early 1900s through about 1995. Cities grew, businesses thrived, and communication flourished through television, radio, newspapers, and books. But if you had a product to sell, a service to provide, or a message to share, once again you ran into a problem. Who among us had the resources for a television station, radio tower, printing press, or publishing house?

Then the Internet came along, and that changed everything.

Today, with a small investment in a domain name and website design, anyone that wants to start a business can do so. This is especially true for a new breed of single-person businesses and solo entrepreneurs — "solopreneurs" for short.

When many people hear the words "entrepreneur" or "startup," they think about icons like Mark Zuckerberg, Steve Jobs, or Elon Musk, or large companies such as Uber, Airbnb, or Instagram. This book won't focus on those kinds of businesses, venture-backed companies with hundreds or even thousands of employees.

Rather, we'll focus on the needs of individuals — coaches, speakers, authors, teachers, and other solopreneurs — who have a unique skill or perspective that can help others. They have the same desire to make an impact in the world that a Facebook or Tesla does, but they also value freedom and lifestyle in their work, and generally operate with minimal infrastructure and support.

The New Titans

Meet Edward Vilga, titan of industry. While some might try and sum up his area of focus in just four letters — yoga — the list of mediums in which he dispenses his creative expertise seems limitless: seven published books (with more on the way), a newsletter, blog, best-selling DVD, group classes, consulting, workshops, social media, and appearances on *Regis and Kelly* and in *People* magazine.

Add to that writing and directing two feature films, five gallery shows, and a play that has toured six continents. We met Edward in our company Mirasee's online course, *Course Builder's Laboratory*, where he was exploring yet another medium, an online course based on his latest book, "The Yoga of Money."

Through his website EdwardVilga.com, the Internet has allowed him to reach millions of people worldwide with his message. But if building your own personal media empire like Edward sounds intimidating, don't be discouraged. Let me introduce you to two very different types of businesses.

Meet Marie Penix, titan of industry. She and her husband wanted to find a unique way to connect with their kids and get them invested in reading while living in the digital age, where it seemed there was nothing but screens in front of their noses. They thought about what connected them with the favorite cartoons from their youth, the games they play now, and the shows they are fans of. It was obvious: It's the *characters*.

Finally, her husband Ben jumped off the couch and said, "What if we could write to our favorite characters and they would actually write back?" A business idea was born, and Marie and Ben now run MonsterTreehouseClub.com, a letter writing service for kids to write to and receive real, handwritten letters back from characters in a book.

Finally, meet Kelli Pearson, titan of industry. Once upon a time she was terrible at math, even failing the same class three years in a row. But then she grew up, learned to love math, wrote some math books, and dedicated several years of her life to making math fun for kids.

"Can you imagine a music class where kids memorized sheet music, but never heard or created an actual note of real music? Of course you can't, that would be crazy. But that's how almost all of us learn math," she says.

Today, through speaking, training, workshops, and downloadable resources on her website, ArtfulMath.com, she helps kids learn math in the way *she* wishes she learned it: with art, play, meaning, and real-world explorations at home and in life.

These modern-day titans are working in different fields, but they all have something in common — their website. While each one has a unique design tailored to their audience, there are seven core elements that form the foundation of their business.

In fact, whether you're a coach or a consultant, a tax attorney or a travel blogger, a vegan or a ventriloquist, you can create and launch your business with some variation of these seven essential pages:

Homepage
About Me
Services
Products
Resources
Privacy
Contact

However, it's not enough to simply *create* the page. There are best practices for each... design and copywriting techniques that will grab the attention of your audience, pique their interest, draw them in with persuasive language, earn their trust, and convert them from casual readers into lifelong fans and customers.

In this book, we'll explain the background and purpose of each page, highlight examples of pages we love, and give you the understanding you need to get your site up and running fast.

And because the web is a visual medium, we've also created some Website Copywriting Extras for visual learners.

Our **Free PDF Resource Guide** is a full-color summary of key takeaways and select website images from the book, while our **online companion course** walks you through the best practices on video, giving you more than 60 minutes of entertaining instruction and showing full color images of our favorite sites.

In tandem with this book, the course gives you an interactive way to learn, a more in-depth level of understanding, and makes it even easier to take action and implement the core concepts so you can create a site that supports your business and your customers.

View the Website Copywriting Extras here:
http://mrse.co/copywriting-extras

Ready to get started? Let's start with the homepage.

Chapter 1: Homepage

Your website's homepage is the hub of your online business, a digital storefront that tells your audience what you do and how you help the world. If you're a titan of industry, consider your homepage your worldwide company headquarters.

The challenge of designing and building your homepage is that it needs to accomplish several things. It should be beautiful to look at, yet easy to navigate. It should build trust and reflect your personality, yet be persuasive and drive people to action.

Co-author Jim specifically remembers the exact moment when he realized how challenging building a great website could be.

I was working in the online games division of ESPN.com

in the late 1990s, when the web was still fairly new. We were updating our homepage and our lead designer, Dan, was walking me through the latest mockup. As he showed me the various elements on the page, I made a few suggestions that I thought were relevant, but I could see that he was frustrated.

I couldn't understand what was bothering him, so I said, "I think it looks great overall! If the design had that one additional element I mentioned, I think it would be absolutely perfect. What's wrong?"

He looked back at me and explained, "Everyone has that one additional element. Ben is the Creative Director, so he's looking at it from a design perspective, and wants to change the colors. Roger and Brandon in editorial think the stories are the most important, so they want the daily articles to be front and center. John in production argued that since people come here daily to access their team, the navigation to that area should more prominent. You'll be shocked to hear that Rick in ad sales asked if we could make the ad banners larger to keep our sponsors happy. Meanwhile, Krish and the engineering team want to make sure all the code is optimized so that the site loads fast and runs great. And finally, James is focused on sales, so he wants the Buy button and call to action to be larger and more obvious. Don't forget that he's the VP of the department and our boss."

I was speechless. Up until that point, I hadn't thought about all the elements that made a website great, and I suddenly had a newfound respect for design and functionality.

Fortunately, a lot has changed as the web has matured. While there will always be tradeoffs and power struggles between design, editorial, sales and engineering, over time a set of best practices has emerged. When you understand and apply the principles in this book, you'll be able to build or improve your website for maximum effectiveness without all the headaches businesses faced in those early days.

Now, something needs to be said here. Your goal is not to build the perfect website. Your goal is to create the best possible website *for your business*. This means taking the concepts you'll be learning and adapting them to suit your own personality, industry, and audience.

Similarly, we can't hope to teach you *everything* you need to know in this book. Not only are the needs of each business uniquely different, but over time technology and platforms and design trends change. However, combining our best practices with your own insight will be enough to launch or grow your business, and give you a solid foundation from which you can adapt and evolve as times goes on.

Website design and framework

If you already have your website up and running and want to jump right in and start optimizing your pages, skip ahead to the Key Homepage Elements section.

But if you're just getting started, let's look at three ways to design and launch your site.

1) Use a WordPress Theme

Our recommended option for building your site is to use WordPress (WordPress.org), a free and open source website publishing system and currently the most popular platform for personal sites on the web by a wide margin.

While WordPress itself is free to install, you'll need to purchase hosting and a domain name. How to do that and opinions on the best hosting platform could fill another book, so check the web for tutorials and how-tos.

On the design side of things, there are thousands of beautiful templates, known as themes, available to get you started. A few sites to explore include WooThemes, ThemeForest, Elegant Themes, and StudioPress.

Pricing varies by site, but generally expect to pay a one-time fee of about $99 for your theme. Themes are usually organized by topic or industry, so you can match the general look and feel to your business, such as travel, consulting, real estate, or photography.

Important tip: When choosing a theme, check to see if the developer is active in updating their themes. This indicates that they're keeping the code up to date with the latest security and design updates, responding to issues that users have found, and are likely around to answer the occasional question you may have that is unique to your site.

The advantage of hosting your own site through WordPress.org is that you own every aspect of the site, and can customize it as your wants and needs grow. You're also able to add plug-ins and third party programs. (Note that this is different from WordPress.com, a free option that offers less flexibility).

While purchasing a theme can quickly establish the look and feel of your site, modifying that theme to make it your own can be a challenge for those who are not technically inclined or don't have the time to do so. If that's the case, you'll want to get some assistance.

2) Hire a designer to create your site

For the solopreneur with a specific vision of what they want their site to look like, or for the person that wants to outsource the creation process and leave it to the experts, consider hiring a designer to create your site.

The advantage is that you'll get a site that is exactly what you want, and hopefully forge a long-term relationship that will allow you to work with the designer to make changes and updates to your site as your business grows and evolves.

The downside is finding the right designer for your needs. Costs to build your site can vary dramatically, from $500 to $10,000 or more. Unlike some of the available themes, which have been purchased by thousands of users, tested out in the wild, and continually updated and supported by a team, you're putting your faith in a single person or agency.

Sometimes a person has a fantastic eye for design, but their coding skills are a little rusty. Other times it's the opposite, your site is light and fast and optimized for search engines, but lacks the visual appeal to stand out in a crowded niche. Not surprisingly, it's often beneficial to hire one person with a UI/UX (user interface and user design) background to design the site, and another person to do the coding.

So how do you find a designer you can trust and who fits your budget? Online, you can use sites such as 99Designs, Freelancer.com, and Upwork (formerly Elance / oDesk), or in person you can reach out to your network for recommendations. Either way, use common sense:

- Be clear about your budget and timeline going into the project.
- View previous work to get a feel for their style.
- Ask to speak with former clients and check for recommendations and testimonials.
- Have a conversation about the goals and

expectations of your project before jumping in, to make sure you're both on the same page.

3) Use an all-in-one solution

If you're looking to get started fast, consider using a service with pre-existing templates that get you up and running quickly. Current solutions include Squarespace, Wix, and Weebly, to name a few.

The advantage of these sites is, for a monthly fee, they take care of a lot of the heavy lifting for you. Most provide the following: beautiful, mobile-responsive design templates, e-commerce integration, photo galleries, drag and drop functionality, blog setup, site statistics, domain names, and site hosting.

The big tradeoff for ease-of-use is that you lose flexibility. If your business needs a very specific page or design element, it can be difficult to integrate it into these one-size-fits-all platforms. Also, some popular products and services such as plug-ins, analytics, A/B testing, learning management systems, social sharing, and blogging tools that can only be used on WordPress-hosted sites.

Finally, these sites might make it more difficult to implement a robust email marketing strategy because they may limit the use of popular third-party tools. For these reasons, if you're running a serious business and you're building your website for the long term, we don't recommend these all-in-one solutions.

Key Homepage Elements

No two businesses are exactly alike, and thus no two websites are exactly alike. What might seem mandatory for an author might be optional for a personal trainer. That being said, here are the elements most commonly found on solopreneur websites:

Hero Image
When someone lands on your website, you better make an impression fast.

Real fast.

As reported in Entrepreneur.com, it takes less than **two-tenths of a second** for an online visitor to form a first opinion of your brand once they've landed on your company's website, according to researchers at the Missouri University of Science and Technology.

During that brief moment in time, they're deciding

what your site is about, if it looks trustworthy, if it's relevant for them, and thus, whether they will stay or leave. To make a good first impression, you'll want a strong visual image, often called the hero image.

Why is the design so important? According to one study reported in ConversionXL.com, 94% of first impression feedback was design-related, while only 6% had to do with the actual content of the website itself. Once you've made a great first impression, you'll have their attention so that they'll explore the rest of the content on your site.

So what kind of image should you use? There are two ways to look at it:

1) It's all about you

Look, it's ok to brag a little bit. We won't judge. And let's be honest, if you're an author, speaker, teacher, expert, coach, or consultant, you're the face of your company. If people are coming to *your* site to get *your* expertise, it's actually a good thing to align their expectations with the results. Hey, if Oprah can put her own photo on each and every cover of her magazine over the last 15 years and have nearly 2.5 million subscribers, then why can't you put your own photo on your website?

Take a look at the websites for some of the top online thought leaders, like Seth Godin, Michael Hyatt, Chris Ducker, Pat Flynn, Derek Halpern, Lewis Howes, Jaime Tardy, Marie Forleo, Jeff Walker, Ramit Sethi, and Michael Port.

They understand that people come to their site to see them, so when you go to SethGodin.com, why shouldn't you see a great photo of Seth Godin?

2) It's all about them

By them, we're referring to your reader, your site visitor, your potential client, the person in the world you were meant to serve. Think less about what you *can do* and more about how you want to *make them feel*.

To see this in action, take a cue from the companies in the "service on demand" economy, such as Uber, Airbnb, Plated, Task Rabbit, or Rent the Runway. When you visit their sites, the hero image is always the *end result* of what will happen if you use their service… a convenient ride, an amazing place to stay, a delicious meal, a day without chores, or a closet full of beautiful clothes.

So if you're a fitness coach, your image might be a healthy person with great abs or a before and after transformation. If you're an organization expert, your image might be an impeccably neat closet.

So how do you decide which method to go with? It's your website, so the choice is up to you. Of course, you could always take the logical approach, design two different pages, and determine the best result through A/B testing or surveys, but the decision is often more art than science. And while you might be ready to launch your first website right now, a helpful exercise is to try and think a year or more into the future.

Let's call this the talk show test. Do you want to be Oprah or do you want to be The Tonight Show? With Oprah, she is the focal point. Whether you're talking about her show, her magazine, or her book club, she's the queen bee. So if you see yourself as a natural entrepreneur, even if you're just launching your first book now, if you see yourself going on to write a series of books, launch online courses, live stream video, or whatever technology is to come, then you should focus on yourself as the brand.

Now look at The Tonight Show. While the format has remained roughly the same for well over 50 years, they've been able to transition from Johnny Carson to

Jay Leno to Conan O'Brien (then back to Leno) and then to Jimmy Fallon. While the host is always featured prominently, there's also an underlying franchise.

So if you're looking to build a long-term brand, one that you might even exit or sell one day, it might make more sense to focus less on yourself and more on your users when naming and designing your site.

Logo

Does your website need a logo? Ask 10 people and you'll probably get 10 different opinions. Some would argue that it's an essential part of any brand, a visual image that you can carry over from your website to your videos to your business cards and other marketing materials. Others would say that it's unnecessary, especially if your brand is "you" and not a company name.

For logo creation, follow the same advice we offered for website design. Look for recommendations within your network for a designer you can trust and who is within your budget, or crowdsource your design using a site such as 99Designs, which we used for this book cover.

Whichever way you choose to go, this much is true: Make sure you have a business before you have a logo.

In other words, many first-time entrepreneurs spend weeks of time and hundreds of dollars worrying about crafting the perfect logo, when what they should be doing first is defining their business strategy and securing their first customers. Having a business card does not mean you have a business.

Tagline

A more crucial element to go along with a logo and your hero image is your tagline, a simple sentence that defines what you do. Here are a few examples:

I help people create & sell digital products & programs online.
- David Siteman Garland, TheRiseToTheTop.com

I'm the crash test dummy of online business, sharing what works (and what doesn't) so you know exactly how to build your business better.
- Pat Flynn, SmartPassiveIncome.com

Be the most memorable person in the room. I'll show you how.
- Vanessa Van Edwards, ScienceOfPeople.com

Take more action in your life or business.
- Jason Zook, JasonDoesStuff.com

Learn everything that personal brand business builders need to know to profit and grow!
- Chris Ducker, ChrisDucker.com

The simple formula for your tagline is "I help [blank] do [blank] by [blank]." For example, "I help busy moms cook healthy meals by providing weekly meal plans to their inbox." We'll learn a bit more about this in the About Me section.

Social Proof

If you follow any online entrepreneur, you've probably noticed a collection of logos with the phrase, "As seen on" and a list of website, magazine, or newspaper logos.

This design element is called "social proof," and serves to give new visitors to your site a quick visual indication that your site is legitimate. As the thinking goes, if you're important enough to have appeared on a large, well-known site, then by extension your site is legitimate as well.

Other sources of social proof include testimonials and reviews from users that have hired you or purchased your products. No one wants to be the first person to try out a new product, so seeing other satisfied customers builds trust.

Email Opt-in

If there's one critical item you should implement on your website as soon as you launch, it's a way to collect the email address of your visitors. If you're just starting out, you might think that it's best to wait until your site has been up and running for a bit before you add this, but it's an easy thing to keep postponing.

We've listened to thousands of podcast interviews with entrepreneurs over the past 10+ years, and when asked, "What is something in your online business that you would had done differently?" a significant number replied, "I would have started building my email list sooner."

That's not to say you should go in without a strategy. Are you going to do a monthly email newsletter? A weekly update with new recipes, coaching advice, networking tips, yoga positions, or the latest tech gadgets? Will you construct an auto-responder series, a pre-written progression of emails that guides a user through valuable content before presenting them with an offer?

No matter what particular strategy you employ, your goal is to build an ongoing dialogue with your site visitors. While various social media platforms have come and gone, email has remained the one constant method by which you can reach a person one-on-one and build a relationship.

Unfortunately, advising on an entire email strategy is outside the scope of this book, but here are the things you need to know:

- Start building an email list as soon as possible.

- Sign up for an email service provider such as AWeber, MailChimp, ConvertKit, Constant Contact, Wishpond, or others. Each one has its pros and cons, which you can review online, but the important thing is to choose one and get started.

- A common practice is to create a free giveaway to offer visitors in exchange for their email. At Mirasee we call this a "first impression incentive," but it's also known as a "lead magnet." This is a piece of content or opt-in offer such as a pdf, ebook, video, checklist, quick-start guide, or free course, that is aligned with the goal of your site. You'll often see email capture wording such as, "Join our newsletter and receive our free resource guide." The visitor enters their email, they get added to your list, and then they automatically receive the content.

- Most email service providers have free widgets (snippets of code) that allow you to embed the email capture area on your website. Another option is a popular service called Leadpages, a paid add-on that allows you to quickly and easily build landing pages and popup boxes for email capture.

Remember, you're never trying to "trick" people into giving you their email address. It's not about the sheer number of subscribers, but rather, connecting with people who truly want to hear from you and your brand. When your product or service resonates, you'll know it.

For example, let's go back to Marie from the Monster Treehouse Club. In pursuit of learning how to market their idea, she stumbled upon Danny's book, *Engagement from Scratch!*. Because she resonated with what he had to say, she started following Mirasee (then known as Firepole Marketing) and joined our email list.

"After reading *Engagement from Scratch!*, we went from 3 people on our email list to 300 after following just a couple of his tips, so I was like, I need this class since I have to get from 300 to 3,000."

Because of the value she got from the book, in the Spring of 2014 she signed up for our *Audience Business Masterclass* online course. She hit her 3,000 subscriber goal in just a few months, but didn't stop there. As of Spring 2016 she's nearing 15,000 subscribers with no signs of slowing down. "We're definitely not a hobby anymore!"

Call to Action

While it's great to have a visitor come to your beautiful website and look around, ideally what you want them to do is take action. What that action is depends on your underlying business strategy. Here are a few ideas:

- For most solopreneurs, the goal is to build your email list. This begins a long-term relationship with a user, so encourage them to sign up for your newsletter or join your mailing list.

- Another call to action (which still might involve collecting an email) could be signing up for a webinar or setting up a phone consultation.

- Sometimes you want the user to consume more content, whether that's reading your most popular blog articles, watching your videos, or subscribing to your podcast.

- And for some, the goal is to be hired, so the call to action might drive people to a "Work with Me" or "Speaker" page.

No matter what the goal, while you want to make it easy for users to navigate your site, don't overwhelm your visitor with too many choices. Instead, gently push them in a single direction.

Blog

Many people mistakenly use the phrase starting a "blog" with starting a "website" interchangeably, but that's not technically correct. A blog is generally an ongoing series of articles or stories that cover a given topic *within* a personal or business website, while a website can stand on its own. You can be a coach, consultant, teacher, speaker — even an author — and launch a very successful online business website using the seven essential pages we'll cover here — without having a blog.

Some people just don't enjoy writing, or it's not a great fit for their business. Others might find that a podcast or video is the best way to present ongoing content, or that LinkedIn.com or Medium.com is a better site to distribute the occasional post. As long as you can give value through your products and services, your website will be enough, even without a blog.

That being said, having a blog on your website has many advantages. One advantage is that your writing is a great way to connect with your readers, so they can get to know your personality and your "voice." Another advantage is that the more content you put out into the world around your niche, the more likely it is for you to rank higher in search engines and for people to find you.

Once again, covering an entire blog strategy is beyond the scope of this book and you'll find countless resources on the web, so add a blog section as the eighth item on your site if it makes sense for your business.

Navigation

Your homepage will need navigational menus to allow users to jump from section to section on your site. You can approach this in many ways, from dropdown lists to expandable "hamburger menus," which are three simple horizontal lines (similar to the bread-burger-bread layers of a hamburger) that let a designer represent a menu on mobile devices with smaller screens.

Additionally, some of the elements we've just discussed should be carried over from your homepage to all of the other pages in your site, such as your company logo, tagline, and email capture functionality.

The key things to know are:

- Make sure your menus are clear and functional across all devices: desktop, tablets, and mobile. Cool hover effects that are easy to navigate on a large screen with a mouse can be frustrating when the links are too close together on a phone.

- Aim to be clear, not clever. While it might be tempting to call your "About Me" link "Moi" since you're like, totally obsessed with French culture, you run the risk or confusing 95% of your visitors who aren't in on the joke. Remember, you only have milliseconds to make a first impression.

- Some great resources for user interaction are the work of Jakob Nielsen, (the guru of webpage usability), at the Nielsen Norman Group, reports and articles from UserTesting.com, and the book *Don't Make Me Think* by Steve Krug.

So what elements will you put on your navigation

menu? The rest of this book will tell you! Keep reading to find out.

Case Study: Michelle Ward

Michelle Ward is the "When I Grow Up Coach," a Brooklyn-based professional coach, author, speaker, teacher, former actress, and ukulele player. She also happens to have a great homepage that hits on just about every element we just covered. So visualize the following and let's walk through it (remember you can download our free Website Copywriting Extras to see images of the actual page).

Design - Michelle's site is built on WordPress and is clean and fast-loading. Her company name and domain name, WhenIGrowUpCoach.com is easy to say, easy to spell, and ties directly into her brand. As she explains, "I help others find their own path, especially 'creative types' who want to find fulfilling work. I help them figure out what they want to be when they 'grow up,' no matter their age."

Navigation - Her menus are clear, leading to pages for Coaching, Speaking, About Michelle, Press, Contact, Blog and Podcast. The site is mobile responsive, so that the navigation turns into a three-bar "hamburger menu" when viewed on a mobile device.

Logo - Michelle's playful logo is a briefcase (representing business), but it's filled with creative items such as a camera, paint brush, clarinet, button, and paperclip. Whether you're into art, music, fashion, or writing, you can identify with one of those symbols.

Tagline - The site's prominent tagline is, "Dream career guidance for the creative woman." In just seven words, she nails the essence of her site, targets her audience, and clarifies four questions a new visitor might have:

1) Is this site for people just looking for an ordinary job? No. It's for people looking for their <u>dream career</u>.
2) Is this site for someone doing research on their own? No. It's for people seeking <u>guidance</u> - or coaching - with their search.
3) Is this site for people with regular office jobs? No. It specifically serves those in a <u>creative</u> field.
4) Is this site for both men and women? No. Sorry guys, Michelle specifically works with female clients.

Image - The main image you see first is a smiling photo of Michelle herself. This makes perfect sense as the business is about her as an expert coach. Other places throughout her site focus on successful students, but someone wanting to learn about coaching will want to see a photo of the coach.

Website copy - While you want to be careful not to overwhelm a reader with too much text, the site does a great job of effectively communicating in three simple paragraphs:

Paragraph 1:
"Do you remember back to being a kid and knowing what you wanted to be when you grew up? Maybe you wanted to be a painter or a doctor or an astronaut-ballerina? Way back when, a dream career was born."

This introduction is effective in that it poses a question and makes the reader think back to their childhood. She's tapping into the beginning of a "hero's journey," which helps in self-selecting her ideal customer. If you didn't have a childhood dream of doing something fabulous, you probably aren't a good client for her services.

Paragraph 2:
"Then you became a "grown-up" and those dreams got

tossed aside. You focused on what was practical and pursued what was safe. You probably bought into the idea that it's called work (and not play) for a reason. But now, you're questioning those truths and thinking that work might not have to be a 4-letter word. That's why I'm here."

In this paragraph she presents the conflict that so many of us have… balancing the path of safe, practical, traditional work vs. play and doing what you love.

Paragraph 3:
"I'm Michelle Ward. As the When I Grow Up Coach, I help creative women like you find a career that is not only financially rewarding, but fulfilling and meaningful too. I don't use magic and I don't read tea leaves,* but I do use a personalized process to help you uncover your lifestyle goals and turn them into your dream career. *But I do play a pink ukulele and I have gone through this journey myself."

In this final paragraph, she brings it back to herself and offers the solution to this conflict. She details who she serves, how she does it, adds her unique personality, and builds trust by saying that she's gone through the same process herself.

Call to action - At the time of this writing, the next image was a call to action, inviting people to a free webinar being held later in the week. Watching a one-hour webinar is a free, easy, low-obligation way for a new visitor to get to know Michelle better.

Infographic-style visuals - While the earlier part of her site relied on text, she smartly uses infographic-style visuals as a fun and easy way to display additional credentials and personality, such as coaching credentials, the most unique career that resulted from her coaching (professional online dating profile copywriter), and fun facts (she won a Judge Judy fan contest and owns two ukuleles).

Social proof - Below the infographic are the logos of the following places she's been seen in: *Forbes, Newsweek, Etsy, The Huffington Post,* and *New York* magazine.

Email signup - And finally, at the bottom of the page is her email newsletter signup form, offering "3 Secrets of Successful Career Changes."

While we're not saying this is the *perfect* website, it has definitely evolved into the perfect website for

Michelle's brand. When she spoke at a conference co-author Jim hosted a few years back, she told the story of how she knew she was on the right track when she first launched her website, which at the time was a bit more fun, with a cartoonish look and colorful pink, green and blue fonts. She created the barebones site, then sent an email to her friends with the link, telling them about her new venture. She got lots of love and support.

She continued, "And then I had a conversation with my Dad. He told me he saw the website and it was great what I was doing, but he wouldn't hire me. My own father!"

So she asked him why not and he said, "Well, the colors, and the tone, and the copy… it's all too casual. It's not professional, and I wouldn't take you seriously if I was a prospective client."

"And while he was saying this, I found myself smiling, which surprised me. I was able to recognize that his advice came from a really good place, because he was a business owner himself and I knew he thought that he was helping me, but I was able to say to him, 'Well Dad, thanks for your thoughts, but I don't want to work with 60-year-old businessmen. I just have to trust that I've put on my site who I am, and the people that are going to want to work with me are going to recognize that.' And it was really validating."

Listening to her gut paid off. "Six months later I got a call from *Newsweek* and they were doing a video feature on life coaching and wanted to interview me. When I told my Dad that, he said to me, 'I know you didn't listen to me to begin with, so keep not listening to me because you're obviously doing something right.' They found me on the Internet."

As her business has grown and evolved, her current design seems to strike the right balance of professional and fun. Of the redesign process, she told me, "This is the 4th iteration of my website since I bought the url in 2008, and the only one where I hired a professional copywriter (my husband Luke!) after working with a branding consultant. The copy is now a direct reflection of the results that came through after working with the consultant. Before that, it was all me and whatever was in my head."

Takeaways

Your website's homepage is the hub of your online business, and it must accomplish several things: create a great first impression, convey your personality, establish trust, inspire action, and make it easy for people to navigate.

If this seems overwhelming, rather than trying to make sure it does *everything*, make sure it's doing *the one thing* you need it to do really well.

In other words, when someone lands on your site, what is the one thing that you want them to do? It could be:

- Enter their email and join your mailing list.
- Set up an appointment or free consulting session.
- Create a deep connection to your brand as they learn more about you, your products, or your services.

If you ask 10 people to look at your site and say, "What is your first impression?" and "What is the first thing you would do?" and you get the results you want, then you're well on your way. But design and branding are not simply a "set-it-and-forget-it" process. As your business and your brand grow over time, continually test and evolve your site to match the changing business environment.

Chapter 2: About Me

"The resume is dead! The bio is king!"

So says storytelling expert Michael Margolis, and if you're reading this book, it's advice you should heed. Sure, those in the corporate world might still need a traditional resume, that tired, outdated, relic of a document that neatly and chronologically details your accomplishments, as if all of life happens in a straight line. But for those of you launching your online business, a compelling story of who you are and what you stand for is of far greater importance.

In most cases, the About Me section of your website is the most visited page after your homepage. Why is that? Because people want to do business with people they know, like, and trust. Creating an effective bio page goes a long way to establishing your brand in the eyes of your potential customer. Here's how to approach it:

Start with your audience in mind

Before you let loose with an exhaustive laundry list of every website you've ever been featured in and every award you've received since childhood, pause and think about the audience you're trying to serve. This seems counter-intuitive — after all, the page is called About *Me* — but it's critical that you frame things from the viewpoint of your reader.

- What's in it for them?
- Who is the audience you serve?
- What are the outcomes you create?
- Who is your site for? And who is it not for?

How did you get here and what do you stand for?

Above all else, your bio should tell a story. Talk about your path, how you started out, and what brought you to where you are now - your hero's journey. Make sure your personality shines through.

Margolis is the founder of Get Storied and he's been helping individuals tell their stories since 2002. He offers a free story-telling mini-course for those just starting out and advises major corporations such as Google, Marriott, and Zappos.

His advice is to lead off your bio by speaking about your point of view: What's the riddle you're trying to solve and what are you really curious about?

"It's great to list the accomplishments and the jobs you've had in your career, but what's important is to connect the dots for me as the reader of why I should care. How does that experience inform or allow you to now do what you're doing?"

He points to media entrepreneur Gary Vaynerchuk as someone with a great "origin story." His backstory (garyvaynerchuk.com/biography) deftly breaks down his background into six stages, but let me summarize and paraphrase his early years:

Gary Vaynerchuk was born in Belarus in the former USSR and immigrated to the US, where the entire extended family shared a studio apartment in Queens. His father began working at a relative's liquor store and eventually moved the family to Edison, NJ. As a young child, Gary began his entrepreneurial career by ripping flowers out of his neighbors' yards and using his natural charm to sell them right back, then upgraded to operating an entire lemonade stand franchise, managing multiple locations and commuting via Big Wheel to collect his profits.

In his early teens, Gary cornered the local market for baseball cards, often making thousands in a weekend with his keen eye for deals and razor-sharp sales tactics. But at the age of 14, Gary's father literally dragged him into the family liquor store business, putting him to work for $2 an hour bagging ice in the basement. Eventually, Gary took the business online at WineLibrary.com, grew the business from $3 million in sales to $60 million in just five years and created a YouTube show called Wine Library TV with more than 1,000 episodes before becoming a prominent speaker, investor, and media entrepreneur.

Don't you immediately feel like you have a fuller understanding of who he is and where he came from? Hard worker. Innovator. Family man. Hustler. Smart aleck. Sales guy. Business builder. Yup, that's Gary Vee.

Tips and Tricks

Cut the jargon - It's great that you "help world-class B2B enterprises synergize across multi-disciplinary CRM platforms," but wait, what the heck does that mean? If your mom can't understand what you do, there's a good chance your audience won't get it, either.

Be self-deprecating - Look, we all know that this whole dance can make us feel like a self-congratulatory blowhard at times. Be humble and don't be afraid to poke fun at yourself to show you're in on the joke.

Add humor … if appropriate - Adding humor to your bio is a great way to reveal your personality and give people a laugh. But don't force it. If comedy just isn't your thing, or if your business deals with more serious topics, don't add a joke just for the sake of having one.

Add your location - One way people instantly try and "place" you is by learning where you were raised or where you live now. For example, you may "Thrive off the energy of New York City," or "Call the rolling hills of Tennessee your home." Maybe you were "Raised in a small town in America's Heartland," or "Are based in the innovative think tank of Silicon Valley." Your location and origin can both lend a particular vibe and feeling to your public persona.

Create 3 versions - As you begin to expand your reach, you might find the need for 3 different versions of your story:

1) A one page bio (for your About page or a "one-pager" marketing handout)

2) A one paragraph bio (for things like speaking gigs)

3) A one sentence bio (for guest post bylines or a Twitter bio)

Add a photo - Have you ever clicked on someone's About Me page and were thinking, "Hmmm… who is the person behind this website?" When the page finally loads and you're greeted with a wall of text, and you realize they don't have a photo, it's a bit frustrating, right? You're looking to make that connection and put a face to the story you've just read about.

Take the opportunity to use a different photo than the hero image on your homepage, one that will further reinforce your branding. A serious business might have you looking confident in a sharply tailored suit. A meditation website might show you relaxed in your garden. A family-focused site might show you surrounded by your adorable children, while a fitness coach might show you pushing it to the limits in the gym. So don't be shy… smile and put yourself out there.

Add a video - To take things a step further, some solopreneurs aren't shy at all and love putting themselves front and center. Filming a quick introduction video to not only show your face and your writing, but to communicate your voice, your presence, and your energy can be extremely effective at making a connection with your users.

The appetite for online video continues to grow exponentially. While stats are changing constantly, here's a snapshot from a moment in time: Between April 2015 and November 2015 alone, the number of daily video views on Facebook doubled from 4 billion to 8 billion. Not to be outdone, just three months later in February 2016, social app Snapchat announced that they were also serving 8 billion video views per day - an increase of 5X from the previous year.

One person who uses video well is author, chef, and on-air personality Kelly Senyei of JustATaste.com. Her video not only shows her skillfully preparing gorgeous spreads of food that will make your stomach rumble, but she

47

effectively tells her backstory by showing a photo of her as a small child in the kitchen. You immediately sense this was something that she was born to do.

Add a quirky hobby - Above all else, your About Me page needs to have personality and be memorable. Are you a triathlete? Obsessed with reality TV? Did you play the tuba in your high school band? It's these little quirks that bond people to you and your story. Margolis himself does this by including his love of chocolate in his bio:

I eat more chocolate than the average human, I throw chocolate tasting parties, I grew up in Switzerland as a kid, and I could talk for hours on chocolate.

He says, "What I find is it's those little things that end up being what people follow up on. When people email me or connect on Twitter, often times their first introduction is like, 'Oh, dude, I love chocolate, too.'"

Related elements to consider

While those are the basic elements of an About Me page — who you are, what you do, and who you serve — there's some additional information you might choose to include to allow the reader to get to know you even further, help them navigate your site, and build additional trust.

The nature of your business and importance of each element will determine if and how you display these additional pages. For example, a Start Here callout might be prominently displayed on your homepage and become its own menu item on your navigation, Testimonials might appear in several places throughout your site, and a Media Kit or Press Page might simply be links in your site footer.

Purpose

This is a newer concept that's similar to your About Me page, but takes things to a different level. A company called Fictive Kin created a page at SlashPurpose.org, with the goal of urging all website owners to create a /purpose page on their site. They write:

"This (/purpose) page exists, because we think the world would be a better place if the people trying to shape it spoke openly and plainly about their vision for the future."

Your purpose page, sometimes called mission or values, might include such items as your driving reason for getting up in the morning, the "why" behind what you do, policies for contributing to the world, charity information, or your broader view for giving back to society.

Start Here Page

Sometimes your site has a lot of different elements such as years of archived blog posts, dozens of videos, multiple topic areas, and an array of helpful resources. While this can represent an impressive body of work, it can be overwhelming to first-time visitors. If you have a complex topic, consider creating a "Start Here" section.

For example, let's say you cover Internet business. There are so many elements to consider: choosing your niche, finding your voice, creating products, serving your customer, and scaling an existing business. If a newbie lands on your site and is confronted by all these topics, they might throw their hands up in confusion and leave. However, a Start Here section can ask a few key questions to find out where they are in the journey, and point them to the most appropriate content to get started. Author and entrepreneur Michael Hyatt has a good example on his site.

Testimonials and Praise

It's a smart idea to sprinkle social proof throughout your site, such as adding a testimonial on your About page, a recommendation on your Services page, and a reassuring quote on a checkout sales page.

However, if your business relies strongly on recommendations and proven results, it might make sense to create a stand-alone page that can be linked to just for testimonials and praise. This page can go deeper into case studies and results, showing images, stats, and even video testimonials.

Media Kit

If you appear often on blogs, podcasts, at events, or in other media, it's helpful to have a central "media kit" page for official press photos, bylines, bios, book covers, social media handles, etc. so people can download them quickly and easily.

Take our math wizard Kelli Pearson. She includes the following resources all in one place for any media outlet looking for information:

- Email address
- Downloadable bio, including "Ten Fun Facts You

Didn't Know About Me"
- Links to her business on eight social media platforms, including a printable version
- Hi-res and low-res versions of her book covers
- A quick description, downloadable synopsis, and free chapter of her book
- Five testimonials plus a downloadable version
- Suggested interview questions in Word and PDF form
- Two hi-res and low-res headshot photos for download

Another similar example is author Marcy McKay, another Mirasee *Audience Business Masterclass* student. She includes the following in her author-centric media kit:

- Short and long version of her book description
- Two author photo options
- Short and long version of her bio
- Four versions of her book cover art
- Four testimonials
- Three awards the book has won
- Twelve sample interview questions
- Email and social media contact information

Press Page

While many sites now just show logos of websites the person has appeared on, displayed with an "As seen on" collage, it's often advantageous, especially for writers or those doing a lot of video, to connect visitors to the actual content.

For example, if your work has been featured in *The New York Times* or on CNN, don't just mention it; link to the specific article or clip. Better yet, save the story as a pdf or screenshot and make it available on your page. This way, you keep visitors on your site, rather than sending them away. It's always good to have your own copy of your press mentions anyway, in case the site decides to take the article down or if the site gets updated and the links break.

Examples

Well-written About Me pages aren't hard to find with a little searching on the web. For example, when we searched for "Examples of great About Me pages" we found several round-up posts highlighting examples that were "the best," "stand out," "groovy," and helped you "get hired," You can narrow things down by searching for examples within your niche, or looking at

About Me pages for freelance copywriters, people who get paid to write About Me pages for other people. (How meta).

Here are a few we found:

Amy Porterfield (amyporterfield.com/about) weaves a great tale of her origin story, how her family played a part in defining who she is, and how you as the reader are brought along her journey. She weaves in the relatable (guilty pleasure of celebs and reality TV), the unexpected (a job at Harley-Davidson?), the social proof (photos with Tony Robbins), and the call-to action (put your email right here). She also has a separate sidebar call-out of her six values, which makes it easy to see and read.

James Clear approaches things a bit differently on his page (jamesclear.com/about). He begins with a big, smiling photo, followed by links to his Facebook, Instagram, and Twitter accounts. He then makes things simple with five "Quick Links," each of which go to the appropriate page on his site.

- Writer on habits and behavior change with over 240,000 email subscribers.

- Photographer covering the culture and habits of people in 20+ countries.
- Teacher sharing the latest research on how to live better via online seminars.
- Keynote Speaker at places like Google and Stanford University.
- Media: Headshot Photo, Speaking Photo 1, Speaking Photo 2.

He then goes into a traditional bio, followed by a call to action to sign up for his email list. After that, he displays testimonials in the form of twelve tweets from people that enjoy his newsletter. We love this tactic because once again, it makes things reader-centric. It's one thing to say "I have a great newsletter" or "People love my newsletter," it's another to actually show other people talking about how much they love it. Then appropriately, he ends with another call to action to sign up for his newsletter.

Highlighting Kelli once again (clearly she excels at both math *and* writing), she takes an educational approach to her About page, since it's such a different subject. Most people think of math as just numbers, but she explains how Artful Math is different. First, after a few intro sentences along with photos of cute children playing (tugging at your heartstrings), she then explains her 5 point math star formula (Magic, Meaning, Mindset, Method, and Mastery), before finally turning the story to her and how she came up with the idea.

Our other titan of industry, Edward, takes a unique approach, separating his background story into an "Authorized bio" and "Unauthorized bio."

Takeaways

Your About Me page is usually the second-most visited page on your site, so it's worth putting some care and thought into making it visitor-focused and personality-driven.

At the conclusion of your bio, make sure you encourage the next steps you want the visitor to take, such as signing up for your email list, subscribing to your newsletter, or exploring your coaching services.

Lastly, don't try to write the perfect bio on the first try. This is a constantly evolving document that you can and should return to on a regular basis as your business evolves. Have fun with it!

For further reading, check out "What Makes a Great About Page" on the Mirasee blog (remember, links to all articles and website examples are listed by chapter on our website at: **http://mrse.co/copywriting-links**).

Now that you've properly introduced yourself to your audience, let's see how to highlight the services you provide.

Chapter 3: Services

There's a single phrase to keep in mind when putting together the Services page on your website:

How do I help people?

Think about all the time you've invested learning and honing your chosen skill, whether that's gardening or programming or golfing. You don't just want to know this skill, you want to share it. So you've taken the time to put together a website. You're gathering a group of like-minded followers, and you're eager and willing to share your knowledge to the world. So ask yourself, how do I help people?

The Services section is generally for listing interactive, personal ways that you can work with and serve your customers to facilitate learning and change.

There are several ways that solopreneurs might title this section, such as Services, Work With Me, or Hire Me. Many people will offer more than one category, and in many cases you'll want to break out a section into its own page, but in general there are four categories to consider:

1. Working 1-on-1
2. Working in groups
3. Speaking
4. Events

Working 1-on-1

If we were to ask you to look back on your childhood and think about a person that made a difference in your life, there's a good chance that you'd come up with the name of a teacher or coach. There are now millions of digital books, blogs, and videos that contain valuable knowledge, but there will always be a place for a true teacher-student dynamic to educate others and share information.

For many solopreneurs, such as a life coach or a nutrition expert, your 1-on-1 clients might be your main source of income, so you're going to want to spend some time perfecting this page. Here are some elements to include:

What are the problems your clients have and how do you solve them?

Take the viewpoint of the visitor first, describing why they are coming to you and the transformation they'll go through after working with you. For example, a nutrition expert might talk about some of the key reasons people seek them out and the way they feel after working with you — having more energy, improved health, sleeping better, and feeling more confident.

What are your qualifications?

Talk about any degrees or certificates you have, additional training, and what makes you qualified to help. A special note here: be very careful when using terms like coach, consultant, certified, and so on. For example, in some cases anyone can call themselves a coach or advisor. In others, terms like therapist or counselor are strictly regulated, so make sure to know the rules within your given area of expertise.

What's it like to work with you?

If someone wants to work with you, how does that look? Is it in person? A series of phone calls? Skype meetings? How often do you meet? What will and won't be covered?

For example, co-author Jim approaches things from two different ways for his side business, Salary Tutor.

The average person has a pretty good idea what to expect if you're hiring a guitar teacher or a personal trainer at the gym, but most people have never even heard of a salary negotiation coach, so it takes a bit more explaining. On my website, one of the elements of my "Work With Me" services page talks about the general *experience* of working with me as a coach. How will it make you feel? Here's what I cover:

What it's like working with Jim:

Purpose – I teach amazing people how to overcome fear, gain confidence, and negotiate their salary so that they can live a more fulfilling life.

My pledge – From our first contact until the moment you jubilantly call with a success story, I want to be the easiest and friendliest person to work with.

Stress-free – Job searching can be frustrating and lonely; negotiation can feel stressful. I'll be in your corner to listen, bring clarity, and ease your fears.

Confidential – Sharing personal financial information requires trust. I place the highest importance on protecting your privacy.

Fun and energetic – Landing your dream job and earning more should be fun! My speaking style has been called "audible caffeine" and I'm told "I light up a room."

Following that, I list two testimonials that specifically speak to those elements (and I link to several more). Once potential clients get a feel for the *experience*, and usually after we've exchanged emails or done an intro call, the second way I approach things is by getting into the *specifics*. For this, I have a prepared PDF document called "What to expect on a 1-on-1 coaching call" which covers the following:

- Goal of the meeting
- Length of the call
- Three phases of the call (Gathering background information, Strategy and planning, Role playing and final summary)
- Frequently asked questions (Email support, billing, referrals, etc.)
- How much of a salary increase to expect
- How to reach me with additional questions

Between both sets of information, clients have a pretty good feel for what the process will be like.

Testimonials

Include a few examples of satisfied clients whom you've worked with 1-on-1. One structure to use is as follows:

- Eye-catching headline
- Introduction
- Results achieved
- Key takeaway
- Signature information

Let's take a look at an example from co-author Jim:

$11,000 increase from a single email

Hi Jim. Thank you so much for all of your help with the salary consulting call. I learned so much in just one session. I sent my counter-offer email based on your recommended structure, and just received their reply.

Result: They increased their offer from $41,000 to $52,000 — an $11,000 raise from just that one email! Additionally, they agreed to give me full benefits for my partner as well.

I am now so excited to begin this new stage of my career, and feel so much better about the move knowing that I'll have almost another $1,000 per month for expenses. Thanks again.

– Vanessa Dalton, San Francisco, CA

Call to action

How do people get started? Fill out a form? Send an email? Make an appointment? Make sure they know how to take the next step.

For some solopreneurs, working 1-on-1 with individual clients or businesses is a less frequent occurrence. For example, a full-time university professor might publish a book, but be available for consulting to private companies a few times per year. Or the CEO of a company might only be available for select clients.

In these cases, the 1-on-1 offer might be phrased as "Individual Consulting" or as co-author Danny calls his service, "Borrow my Brain," and only be available at a very high rate. Some charge $500 an hour or more, or $5,000+ for an entire day.

Working in Groups

In order to reach more members of your community at once, many solopreneurs teach in groups. This could be group conference calls, video hangouts, Facebook groups, Slack channels, or in-person masterminds.

In this section, talk about the value of being in a group setting and the value students get from learning from each other. And again, delve into the details such as how often the group meets, what topics are covered, and what is expected from each individual.

For example, Stella Orange is the founder and creative director of StellaOrange.com, an agency that helps people doing good work get their writing projects done faster, bolder and more profitably.

While she has worked with both individual clients and million dollar companies, one of her most successful projects is her "Write Club," an online writing group for business owners around the world.

On the first three Mondays of every month, the group gets together via video conference for "Shut Up & Write," a 90-minute focused writing session to work on projects such as blog posts, promotional emails, or web copy. They also have access to recorded training on copywriting skills and projects, and a chance to get their questions answered on calls and in a private group.

"I didn't expect this to be so popular, because it seems so simple," Stella says. "For my students, it's a way for them to be held accountable as they actually sit down and do their work. For my business, group training allows me a consistent monthly income and make a greater impact than working 1-on-1."

So whether your group meets face-to-face or on Facebook, give the details on your Services page.

Speaking

As your expertise within a given topic deepens and the awareness of your knowledge within your niche grows, more and more people will want to hear your message. As you expand past working with people 1-on-1, an effective way of reaching others is through public speaking.

Many authors dream of giving a TED talk that reaches millions of people, or getting paid thousands of dollars for each personal appearance. But if the thought of standing in front of a live audience is already making your palms sweat, don't worry. Before we get ahead of ourselves, know that it's ok to start small.

If you're an expert on non-toxic cleaning products in the home, your first "speaking gig" might be presenting to a group of parents in someone's house on a Saturday afternoon. If your niche is providing organizational tips for those looking to live a minimalist lifestyle, you might present to a civic group in your town that is looking for an interesting topic for their monthly meetings. If your expertise ties into a bigger topic, you might be asked to serve on a panel with other "subject matter experts" at a conference.

But as your confidence and audience grows, opportunities to spread your message, help others, — and even get paid along the way — could appear.

There are several key elements you will want to include in your Speaking section.

What topics do you speak about?

Describe the key message that you deliver, focusing on showing how your speech provides value to the intended audience. If you have more than one topic, organize them with the speech title and a brief description so that the event organizer can determine the best fit for their group.

Testimonials

If a group or company is going to pay you to speak, they want social proof from others that you're going to do a good job. Testimonials from the organizers of previous events can go a long way in instilling that confidence, especially if they note that you are easy to work with, are reliable, and provide real value to the audience. Bonus points for being voted the most popular speaker at a conference, or for being invited back multiple times.

Downloadable Speaker 1-Sheet

While much of our work is done online today, there are still many cases where a physical document can provide real value. If you're serious about speaking, consider creating a 1-page PDF that summarizes your services. It would contain many of the same elements listed here (photos of you speaking, popular topics, testimonials), and it makes it easy for an event organizer to print out the page and discuss it with a committee during a meeting, forward it to someone via email, or to use as a leave-behind for your in-person meetings.

Technical Requirements

Speaking logistics don't have to be tricky — just stand up and share your story with a small group of people

— but it can sure get complicated fast. If you have specific needs around microphones, audio speakers, projectors, Wi-Fi connections, or recording your presentation on video, detail them in a bullet list or create a separate PDF. It's easy to make assumptions — until the first time you show up to an event and the organizer says, "Wait, I didn't know you were using slides, we don't have a projector here."

Schedule of past and future events

A list of past events highlights the places you've spoken before, showing social proof and giving people an idea of the events and organizations you work with. Meanwhile, a calendar of future events lists where people can see you speak.

Video of you speaking

While this seems like the most obvious thing in the world, you'd be surprised at how many people skip this step. Imagine this conversation:

You: "I'd love the opportunity to speak at your event." Them: "Great! Where can I see an example of past speeches you've done?" You: "Ummmmmm."

Clearly if you're to be considered a high quality speaker — and especially if you're charging money — people are going to want to see an example of your speaking style and content. Because of this, early in your career, it's often smart to accept opportunities that might not pay as well (or at all) in order to get high-quality video of your speech for use on your website.

Co-author Jim spoke about the topic of solopreneurs making the jump to becoming speakers with Mitch Joel, President of global media agency Mirum (mirumagency.com), and a speaker that has shared the stage with Bill Clinton, Richard Branson, Malcolm Gladwell, and Tony Robbins. On the subject of Speaker pages, Mitch had this to say:

"The amazing thing is, because there's so few people who have a great Speaker page, I think the ones who do it will jump ahead because it's such a rarity. To get somebody to let you up on stage and deliver a keynote or a presentation or be on a panel that engages a Twitter-crazy, iPhone-nuts audience, you have to let them know you're alive. You have to let people know you want to speak. And it boggles my mind how few people do this."

Mitch offers additional tips in his post, How to Market Yourself as a Speaker, and you can check out his speaker page as an example (all links from the book available here: **http://mrse.co/copywriting-links**).

As you can see, there are many elements that could be listed under speaking opportunities. If speaking becomes a major element of your business, you might want to move this section out of your "Work With Me" page and have it as its own link from your homepage.

Events

Do you run events as part of your interaction with customers?

This could be as simple as a weekly Meetup group to foster community and answer questions in your area of expertise, or as large as Chris Guillebeau's annual "World Domination Summit," or as unique as Chris Ducker's "Tropical Think Tank" gathering in the Philippines.

Your Services page is a great place to highlight the events you run or participate in, and collect emails to let people know when tickets go on sale. However, in most cases any kind of significant event will have its own website or subdomain, which you can link to.

For example, on Chris Guillebeau's personal site, rather than having a Services page, he has a specific Events tab on his navigation. On that page, he highlights his 30-city book tour (which is certainly quite an event), his World Domination Summit conference, and his Pioneer Nation workshop.

Taking that one step further, you can click a link and continue on to WorldDominationSummit.com, which is a stand-alone website with all the necessary information for that event.

So as you can see, how you organize things really depends on the size and scope of the events that you host for your business.

Takeaways

Your Services page, also known as Work With Me or Hire Me, is a critical page for many solopreneurs, especially coaches or consultants that often work 1-on-1 with clients.

The goal of the page is to inform the reader what the experience and the details of that interaction will be like, whether it's a personal meeting or a speech for hundreds of people. If speaking or events become a major part of your business, most entrepreneurs add a separate page exclusively for this topic.

Now that we've covered the ways a site visitor can work with you in a personal setting through your services, it's time to explore the best way to offer digital and physical products such as online courses and books.

Chapter 4: Products

In the previous chapter, we remarked how nothing can match the 1-on-1 interaction of a teacher imparting their knowledge to a student. And while that may be true, there's one limiting downfall to that format: scale.

In offering your services, it can be incredibly gratifying to make a difference in someone's life. But as you help more and more people, you run into the issue that there is only one of you and only so many hours in the day, and you start to hit your limit.

That's where products come in as a complement to your services. They're a great way to reach a wider audience, while still infusing your knowledge and personality.

These creations, such as books, courses, apps, and videos, have many advantages:

- While it might take significant time to create a product, once complete it can serve as an asset that can be sold and delivered over and over again with no additional effort, except for the occasional update
- You can reach a broad audience with a consistent message
- Digital products can be delivered instantaneously at little or no cost
- Products can be priced low to reach a mass audience that might not be able to afford your 1-on-1 coaching rate, or priced higher if they provide significant value

Let's look at some of these in detail.

Courses

Online courses are a great way to extend your message and serve your audience. What's great is that you can start simple and expand the breadth of the content within your course as your experience grows. For example:

- A course can be a simple series of videos consisting of audio voiced over PowerPoint slides, along with PDF worksheets. Co-author Danny's course *Write Like Freddy* used this method, delivering four 15-minute videos containing mostly text that walked people through the step-by-step method of becoming a prolific guest blogger, along with a few downloadable templates. A few years later he updated the design, expanded the course, added video, and renamed it *Standout Guest Posting.*

- The companion online course to this very book complements this text-only medium by having engaging videos walking you through the 7 webpages, displaying full-color visuals of websites that we mention, and providing downloads and key takeaways that can be saved or printed.

- For his flagship salary negotiation courses, co-author Jim went all in. Not only did he deliver his content as host, along with some motion graphic animations, but he hired Improv-trained actors to illustrate scenarios a student might face in a showdown between a job-seeker and the "Evil HR lady." Additionally, he included downloadable resources for key research, helpful articles, and a customizable template in PowerPoint,

Photoshop, and Excel format that can be used in an interview to secure the highest salary.

- And finally at the highest end, not only does Mirasee's *Course Builders Laboratory* mix video, audio, and downloadable resources, but we also provide a personal coach for each student (yes, a live person) to guide them through the process.

While it's easy to get carried away and picture yourself as the next Steven Spielberg, adding special effects and shooting video on location, we want to be clear: You should use the simplest and most effective delivery method that gets the job done.

Your Products page is a great place to introduce your courses, and you'll want to present this information based on the format and delivery method you've chosen.

Some services like Teachable, Ruzuku, Kajabi, and Thinkific provide a platform to allow you to host your own online course material, or "school." Others like Zippy Courses, Lifter LMS, Sensei, WP Courseware, and LearnDash are built using WordPress as their underlying platform. Lastly, sites such as Udemy and

Lynda serve as a marketplace to sell your courses to a broader audience. (We link to each platform here: http://mrse.co/copywriting-links).

Some of these sites offer robust design elements, and allow you to customize your domain name so that site visitors can't even tell that they are hosted by a different company. In those cases, you might choose to have your "Products" or "Courses" navigation menu direct right to those pages.

In other cases, you'll want to describe your course on your Products page.

Elements you'll want to include are:

- Description of the course and how it will help the user, including how long the course will take to complete, what the benefits are, and what they'll gain by the end of the course
- Course preview video, which acts a bit like a movie trailer
- Screenshots of what the course looks like so they can get a feel for it before they buy
- Testimonials or reviews from other users
- Information on pricing

Let's look at how this might be arranged on a few levels from body language expert and instructor Vanessa Van Edwards at Science Of People.

On her main product page (she's decided to have fun and simply call the page "Awesome"), she has a summary of her four main courses, The Power of Body Language, Master Your People Skills, The Body Language of Love and Dating, and Body Language for Entrepreneurs.

Each course has 4 elements:
- A one-sentence description
- Three bullet points
- A one to two minute course preview video
- A call to action button to preview this course

Below that she has 5 general testimonials talking about the effectiveness of her courses.

This initial page allows the visitor to quickly assess what course they might be interested in, whether it's an entrepreneur looking for body language tips when presenting a killer pitch, or a hopeless romantic looking for flirting tips while searching for their soulmate. (Wait a minute, what if an entrepreneur wants to find their soulmate?).

Once a user clicks on a course, it goes into a much more in-depth breakdown of what the user will get. She breaks this down under the following headings:

- Do you know what your body language is saying?
- Why Body Language? (with a sample video from the course)
- Does it really work?
- Who is this course for?
- What does this course cover? (with a sample video from the course)
- What This Course Is Not (with a sample video from the course)
- How to Be A Human Lie Detector (with a sample video from the course)
- Lying Myths (with a sample video from the course)
- Other benefits
- Pricing details
- Call to action to buy
- Why me (her bio)
- Second call to action

While your course descriptions will vary, you can see how you can pick and choose from many of the items above that Vanessa has used. The underlying copywriting elements hold true: Spark interest, answer potential objections, target the right customer by saying who your product is — and is not — for, give examples, provide social proof, and then ask for the sale. (Reminder, you can check out our online companion course via our Website Copywriting Extras for a visual walkthrough of the actual page).

Books

There's no doubt that we love our electronic devices. A 2015 study by consulting firm Deloitte showed that Americans collectively check their phones *8 billion times* a day, with the average person glancing 46 times and some age groups checking in far more often than that.

And yet, the book survives. That's not to say the traditional publishing industry has remained the same. Authors are writing books differently (often self publishing), shoppers are buying books differently (forgoing bookstores for Amazon.com), and fans are reading books differently (on Kindles, laptops, and that ever-present mobile device), but the thirst for knowledge continues.

Much like the Speaker section we covered in the last chapter, if you're already an established author, then

"Book" might live on its own section of your website — or even on its own site — instead of under the Products section.

But if you have multiple books, ebooks, or digital downloads, your Products page might be good jumping off point. Let's look at some examples.

Co-author Danny keeps things simple. On Mirasee's Products page, which we call "How We Help," he features his 3 main books, showing the book cover, a short description, and a link directly to Amazon.com.

Co-author Jim has more of a traditional book landing page, using the following elements:

- A photo taken with a group of people at a book event
- An intro paragraph and image of the book cover
- Bullet list of what the reader will learn (using bullets is a great way to break up large chunks of text on a website and adds readability)
- A photo of a woman holding the book in a bookstore (Fun fact: This was taken the very first day my book hit stores. As a first time author, I rushed to my local Barnes and Noble to see my

book on the shelf, and found this nice woman searching for a book around my topic. She ended up buying it, and I asked if I could snap a photo of what might have been the very first person to buy my book.)

- Two testimonials and a link to read more
- Call to action button to purchase on Amazon
- Video book trailer

Jeff Goins is not only an author himself, but teaches other writers how to become authors. On his main site, GoinsWriter.com, he keeps things simple by offering four elements: Email signup, testimonials, a link to his blog, and a link to his book.

For his latest book, rather than describe it on a Products page, he links to a separate website dedicated just to the book itself, ArtOfWorkBook.com. Within that site, you can see the same elements that you might include on your book page:

- An intro video, along with some free bonuses
- Description of the book and the promise it aims to deliver
- Book cover (shown on an e-reader, mobile device, and as a physical book)

- Photo of the author, bio, social media links, and social proof logos
- Endorsements from other authors (and impressive ones at that, Steven Pressfield, Seth Godin, Michael Hyatt, Chris Brogan, Jon Acuff, and Chris Guillebeau)
- One-click icons for sharing on social media
- Link for press inquiries

As you can see, there are many different ways to approach book information. Whether it's on your Product page or a standalone website, many of the key elements are present. And remember, strive for progress, not perfection… your website will evolve over time.

Apps and Other Digital Media

There are many other creations that could fall under the Products category. This could include smartphone apps, WordPress plug-ins, PDF downloads, spreadsheets, Photoshop templates, or video tutorials.

These can be delivered in various ways, from free email downloads to simple e-commerce sites such as Gumroad.com.

Gumroad's website features several diverse examples of creatives that are able to sell their work directly to their fans. Musicians can sell songs, even using a "pay what you want" model. Comedians, serious actors, and documentarians are able to sell their films. Authors can sell books. There's even an online course by someone named Alison Faulkner, who calls herself the ambassador of awesome, that teaches people how to make the perfect sugar cookie with royal icing. Sounds awesome to me.

One prominent example is entrepreneur Nathan Barry. Back when Apple released iOS 7, he put out a guide to help creatives design for this new operating system. He packaged together multiple forms of media and offered several tiers for his App Design Handbook:

- Ebook
- Ebook + templates
- Ebook + templates + videos

The combination of packages he created is not only a lesson in copywriting, but also in marketing strategy. If you think about buying an ebook, most readers are used to paying between $3 and $15 on

Amazon. But Nathan wanted to charge a much higher premium - $39. How was he able to do that?

First, he focused on the value he was delivering. If you buy the latest teen vampire thriller to read on your Kindle for $2.99, it can bring you a few weeks of guilty-pleasure reading before you go to bed. But what Nathan was positioning is that learning a skill for your job or personal business — app design — could return a huge multiple on your investment. Adding mobile development to your resume could lead to a job with a much higher salary, and having your own app can bring in revenue many times over your $39 investment.

The second strategy in place here is called anchoring. By combining other valuable elements — existing templates and video tutorials — and pricing the overall package at $249, now users aren't comparing a $3 ebook against a $39 ebook (four times higher), they're comparing the book as the affordable option to the higher $249 "anchor" price for the top package.

Nathan's thoughts behind this strategy and the tests he ran are detailed as a case study in the blog post, "An eBook pricing model that resulted in $100,000 in sales" (all links from the book are available here: **http://mrse.co/copywriting-links**).

Physical Products

What if you're a solopreneur selling non-digital products? Your Products page acts as your very own storefront to educate visitors, sell them on the benefits, and encourage them to buy.

Let's revisit Marie at the Monster Treehouse Club. Recall that she and her husband wanted to get children away from screens and back to the art of writing and reading. On her Products page, which she hosts on Shopify, she begins with a full color spread of what the child will receive. This includes:

- One book with a main character
- One matching activity book
- T-shirt with that character
- DVD of the Monster reading the book and fun learning activities
- Wristbands
- Trading cards
- Pens
- 3D art project

By showing a photo of these items, a buyer instantly gets a feel for all the products they will be receiving. She even includes the Priority Mail box they'll arrive in, complete with a monster-themed address label. That means she's not only showing what a child will get, but how they'll get it. It's in these details that raving, returning customers are made.

Takeaways

While the services you provide can reach people with a personal touch, physical and digital products allow you to reach a broader audience with your message. The most common ways to do this are through online courses and books, but can also include videos, apps, downloads, and products that are shipped to customers.

When presenting your products, your goal is to follow a structure similar to your About Me page. Begin with the customer in mind by showing the benefits, then describe what they'll receive and the experience they'll have with your product, sprinkle in some social proof, and encourage them to buy.

By now, you're well on your way to telling the world

who you are and what you do. In the next chapter, we'll cover the tools you use to get the job done with a Resources page.

Chapter 5: Resources

Every profession has unique tools to do their job, and people are usually curious what they are. What kind of guitar does my favorite musician use? What brand and model of cleats does the world's top soccer player wear? What about the knives and cookware of celebrity chefs?

Think about the world of entertainment. On the red carpet at award shows, there's usually the question of which designer dress or tuxedo an actress or actor is wearing. Watch aficionados want to know if James Bond is wearing a Rolex or an Omega in the latest spy thriller. Even the evil Joker once quipped, "Where does he get those wonderful toys?" as Batman escaped his clutches once again.

If your business serves as an inspiration to what your readers want to become, many of them will be interested in the day-to-day tools you use to do your job as well, even if you're not a celebrity. For example, if you teach people how to do home renovations on a budget, readers will want to know what's in your toolkit — literally.

Your website's Resources page is the place to list them.

There are four ways to think about items to list on your Resources page:

1. Items you use to <u>run</u> your business
2. Items you use while <u>performing</u> your business
3. Items you use in your <u>personal</u> life
4. Items your reader can use to help <u>their</u> business

Note that you don't want to have a laundry list of each and every product and service that you use — it will depend on what you do. Think about your audience and what will give them value.

For example, if you give financial planning tips for new parents, they might want to know what online bank you recommend, but not what WordPress template you used on your website. If you're a running coach for first time marathoners, they might want to know your personal nutrition plan, but not what accounting program you use. Consider the four categories below, and adjust accordingly.

1. Items you use to <u>run</u> your business

No matter what your niche, if you're building an online presence for your business, there are tools that are needed behind-the-scenes to get the job done.

Website design - Hopefully this book has helped you put the finishing touches on creating an awesome online presence. People want to know how you did it. If you hired a professional designer, give them a shoutout on your Resources page and link to the person's company in your footer. If you used a WordPress theme that was perfect for your business, let people know where to find it. If you created your site with an all-in-one package such as Squarespace, let them know. Perhaps you ran a contest on 99 Designs to create the perfect logo. You know what to do.

Hosting - Along with the look of your site, there are countless options when it comes to hosting. Companies you might have heard of include GoDaddy, Bluehost, DreamHost, and HostGator.

Email - Earlier in this book we talked about the importance of building an email list of your audience. If you're a food blogger, ideally your readers are thinking something like, "I really love the informative emails I get every single Sunday with meal ideas for the week, and the special menus that arrive just in time for the holidays." Their next question might be, "I wonder how they manage all the emails they send?"

Popular email hosting companies include AWeber, MailChimp, ConvertKit, Constant Contact, and Infusionsoft. There are also several ways to *capture* those email addresses. Helpful tools include landing page generators like Leadpages, popup boxes such as OptinMonster, add-ons like Hello Bar, and all-in-one solutions such as Wishpond.

Audio and Video Production - Do you host a podcast, offer online courses, or create videos on YouTube or Periscope? People go crazy wondering what goes into the technical production of this content. They love seeing the behind-the-scenes gear.

Sometimes people are just curious, wondering if you use an iPhone or Android phone to record your daily video update. Others want to know every last product detail and model number from your online course film shoot, including the lighting setup, green screens, microphones, cameras, teleprompters, and editing software.

Administrative Tools - The back-end tools you need to run your business aren't always sexy like the latest digital camera, but they're a necessary part of your work. How do you manage your billing and invoicing? Popular sites include FreshBooks, Harvest, Xero, and QuickBooks. Was it difficult setting up an LLC? Some companies use a lawyer their brother-in-law recommended, while others start with an online service such as LegalZoom.

2. Items you use while <u>performing</u> your business

While every solopreneur business needs a website, hosting, and email provider, there are also resources that are unique to your specific business. Within your given niche, your readers are going to trust your recommendations on the products you use and endorse.

Let me give you an example of the difference between resources for someone running a business vs. someone performing their business. For instance, there are now millions of people using online video. You could be an interior design expert or a life coach and use online video as another way to connect with your audience and extend your brand. It's one of the tools you're using within your business.

Now take the example of Gideon Shalwick, an entrepreneur and marketing expert in the online video space. For Gideon, online video IS his business. On his main website, he covers the latest developments in online video marketing techniques.

When you look at his Resources page (gideonshalwick.com/resources), he starts out by listing the items we just talked about, such as his hosting and email marketing providers. But then he delves into the tools and resources he personally uses to do his job:

- Video Recording Equipment
- Video Hosting
- Video Editing Software
- Outsourcing (Resources for hiring)
- Books
- Additional Tools (Teleprompter software, etc.)

What is unique about his page is the way he breaks down his video recording equipment into three categories:

- Entry Level (What I started with)
- Mid Range (What I used previously)
- High End (What I use now)

There are two reasons why this is incredibly valuable for his readers. First, there is something powerful about reading the phrase, "This is what I use now." If someone has put in significant time and effort in learning their craft, why should a newbie reinvent the wheel? Instead of spending weeks evaluating products and doing all the research, if this is a trusted source, you can simply save time and say, "I'll just use whatever technology he recommends." It also builds trust that the person is endorsing products he actually uses, not because of a sponsor relationship or affiliate income.

And second, it's valuable because he breaks down his camera, microphone, lighting, and voice recorder recommendations into different experience levels. This allows users just getting started to come in at a budget level that's appropriate, and experts ready for high end DSLRs and lenses to use the best option.

3. Items you use in your <u>personal</u> life

One of the adages in business you may have heard is that customers buy things from people they know, like, and trust. Part of that equation is your level of expertise within your given niche… does this person have the experience necessary to teach me what I need to know. However, if you're just focusing on the business side of things, you're only seeing half the picture.

The other half of the success equation is that people also want to know you as a person. As you saw in the About section, infusing personality is a key element for your business. In addition to learning about the products you use in your work, they also love to learn about the items you use in your personal life.

No matter what your profession, is there a product or service that you obsess over or can't live without? Here are some ideas:

- Maybe you were a business traveler for years, lugging 10-pound laptops around, and now the 2.03-pound, 12" Macbook has changed your life.
- Are you a yoga fanatic that only wears clothes from Lululemon?

- Are you a voracious reader, and your Amazon Kindle Paperwhite never leaves your side?
- Do you work from loud coffee shops and swear by Bose noise-cancelling headphones?
- Do you start your day with a particular smoothie with particular ingredients mixed in a particular blender?
- Is there a smartphone app few people know about that you use every single day?

Here's a specific example:

According to his website, James Clear "studies successful people across a wide range of disciplines — entrepreneurs, artists, athletes, and more — to uncover the habits and routines that make these people the best at what they do. Then, I share what I learn in my popular email newsletter."

On his website you can see articles about habits, books about habits, and his newsletter about habits. But then there's one additional link that might seem out of place: Ultralight Travel.

What's listed here is an incredibly organized, epic 6,861-word post listing James' gear recommendations for traveling. He covers everything from backpacks and tech gear to underwear and toiletries. There's even an entire paragraph about titanium sporks.

If you're the type of person that curbside checks the biggest suitcase they can carry, filled with several pairs of shoes "just in case," then this article probably won't appeal to you. But if you're a person looking to live a more efficient life — the exact type of person James wants on his email list — then he's made an instant bond with you. You're either going to come away thinking, "He's just like me" or "This guy is a nut."

It's up to you to decide if information like this should live on your Resources page, your About page, or on its own page like James did (some people title it "Stuff I Love)," but no matter where it is, it's a great way to bond with your audience.

4. Items your reader can use to help their business

While it's important to give your users a peek behind the curtain to see the resources you use to build your site, do your job, and make you unique, remember that when it comes to building a successful business, it's not about you, it's about your reader.

To that end, your Resources page can also focus on the additional tools your ideal customer can use to succeed.

Take the example of Cliff Ravenscraft, the "Podcast Answer Man." For Cliff, podcasting is both his passion and his business. What started as a hobby in 2005 when he was podcasting about the TV show *Lost,* turned into a full-time career producing more than 3,000 episodes for 20 different shows by the end of 2015. He now earns well over six figures as a coach, consultant, and speaker for all things podcasting.

While he highlights the standard items on his Resources page (podcastanswerman.com/resources), such as his website and hosting, the first thing he does is link to his Podcast Training page and Podcast Equipment page. Ultimately, these are the items that his user truly wants… not to learn about *his* business, but to learn how to start *their* business.

Another example is entrepreneur, author, and social media strategist Amy Porterfield. Her Resources page (amyporterfield.com/marketingresources) links to recommended tools for Training, Business, Product

Creation, and Social Media. It's interesting to note that while the Facebook Training 101 listing links to her own "JumpStart Your Facebook Marketing" course, her recommendations for creating courses, LinkedIn, Pinterest, and YouTube link to other industry experts. While some might view this as linking to competitors, it can also be seen as linking to partners. Because Amy is confident in her business, she is comfortable recommending the best possible training for her readers because it is bringing them value.

Another slightly different example is the list of resources that Artful Math uses. Considering that the audience is young children, it makes sense that their resources are about math, not marketing. They include the following "Free Math Printables":

- Fraction strips
- Integer number lines
- Multiplication charts
- Pattern blocks
- And several others

Earning Income From Your Resources Page

Your Resources page is a great opportunity to provide helpful information and insight to your website visitors. But it's also a great opportunity to provide something valuable to you: Income.

Through affiliate marketing — receiving referral commissions for recommending a product or service — you can earn additional income for linking to the resources that you use.

Here are the basics:

1) Companies offering an affiliate program allow you to register with them as a partner.

2) You receive a specific link, code, ID, or URL that is unique to you, so that they can credit any sales directly to your account.

3) Affiliates may be large corporations, small businesses, or individual Joint Venture (JV) partners. Sometimes companies set the same commission percentage for all partners, while in other cases it can vary based on relationships or

sellers that bring in significant revenue or volume.

4) As a partner, when you mention the product or service, you use your unique link or mention your specific code for your visitors to use.

5) When your visitor clicks through the link to purchase the product or service, it doesn't cost them anything more, but the company will pay you a percentage of the sale as a "thank you" for referring the business.

For example:

- As a member of Amazon's affiliate program, you earn a commission when someone purchases your book through a link on your site.

- When recommending AWeber as your email hosting platform, you get paid for each person that signs up for the service.

- You do a joint venture deal with a partner selling a social media training course, and earn a 50% commission for each person that enrolls in that training.

- You have a paid sponsor for your blog or podcast, and when someone enters your promo code at checkout, they receive a discount and you earn a commission.

In fact, for some entrepreneurs, this is a major source of their income. Take the case of Pat Flynn of SmartPassiveIncome.com. In teaching people how to launch an online business, he put together helpful blog posts and YouTube tutorials showing how to set up their website hosting.

According to his public earning reports, in 2014 alone he earned $424,800 just from affiliate commissions for hosting company BlueHost.com. Combine that with his recommendations for landing pages ($59,000 from Leadpages), email ($22,000 from AWeber), website themes ($15,000 from Thesis theme for WordPress), and training programs ($20,000+ from several partners), and you can see that the numbers can add up fast.

However, lest you get greedy or jealous, think twice before you view your customers as a get rich quick scheme. Pat's results are far from typical, and he has been providing value and serving his audience since 2008. He is incredibly transparent in sharing his income - and his expenses - and his body of work is right there on the web for all to see.

Still, affiliate income can be a sticky subject. To be clear, there is nothing wrong with earning a commission from your recommendations. But there are two factors to consider — ethics (which we'll cover below) and legal (which we'll cover in the Privacy Policy section).

In order to earn the trust of your customers, they must believe you are ethically acting in their best interest, and the best way to do that is through transparency. Gideon Shalwick was clear when he stated, "This is the equipment I used to use," and "This is the equipment I use now." On James Clear's Ultralight Travel page he states, "This page shares my complete ultralight packing list, my favorite pieces of travel gear, and my thoughts on why it's better to travel the world with just one bag." It's easy to see that this is gear he not only endorses, but has used in his travels to more than 20 countries.

Likewise, sometimes it's important to be transparent when you *haven't* used the product. Often you'll hear an author interviewed about their new book on a podcast, and the host will remark, "Unfortunately I haven't had a chance to read this latest book, but I have read your previous work and it's amazing and I always learn something new, so I urge my listeners to go grab a copy."

Here are three ways that you can be transparent about affiliate links:

1) Somewhere on your Resources page, add a disclosure. For example:

"Note that the products listed contain affiliate links, on which I earn a commission. This does not cost you any more money, but allows me to earn extra income to support my business. I have tested, used, and endorse every item on this list in the production of my business."

2) Use affiliate disclosures inline within a blog post or resource listing when you want to be explicitly clear. For example:

"Last week I interviewed Marie Forleo about her <u>B-School training program</u> (affiliate link) and it's a great option for growing your business."

3) Create a central affiliate disclosure listing page, which you can link to throughout your site. This can include things like your affiliate policy, site sponsors, and companies you invest in or that invest in you. See the Privacy Policy section for more information.

While it's important to be transparent around these issues, you don't need to be apologetic. If there's a product or service that you absolutely love… one that makes your job easier, is a pleasure to work with, and is a great match for your readers, then by all means, shout it from the rooftops.

One final note we have to add is that disclosure laws change often, and we're not lawyers, so you need to do your own research and consult with your legal advisors regarding your particular business.

Takeaways

Your Resources page can be an incredibly valuable page on your website, providing insight to visitors about the tools you use in your business and personal life and giving them recommendations for helping to grow their business.

Additionally, through affiliate programs, your recommendations can serve as a source of revenue when the offers are presented ethically and transparently.

Great work! We're nearing the home stretch. In the next chapter we'll quickly cover some legal issues and your site will be close to finished.

Chapter 6: Privacy

Admittedly, after telling the world your unique story, sharing your creations, and describing how you help others, wading through the legalese of privacy policies and terms of service isn't much fun.

But if you're serious about doing business in the digital age, this section provides a level of trust and clarity to your readers and customers, and puts policies in place to protect your business — *before* something happens.

Sadly, we live in a litigious society so it's important for you to protect yourself and your business assets by doing the necessary due diligence for your site. Likewise, we need to state the obligatory, "We are not lawyers," so please view the following as general recommendations, but consult your own legal counsel.

Part of the difficulty in this area is finding accurate information online. The most conservative attorneys and websites preaching that you need an extensive terms of service page that is updated every six months, are also the ones who, (surprise!) make money from you every time you update that policy. Meanwhile, those that say "don't bother" might be small players with nothing to lose, so always consider the source.

In the Resources chapter we talked about the ethical side of affiliate links, making sure you are transparent with your users and letting them know you are earning a commission. But there's also the legal side, guidelines set by the Federal Trade Commission around online business practices (note that these are guidelines subject to fines, not laws). The original guidelines for bloggers were released in 2009 and were updated in 2013.

The website at FTC.gov offers information on the following:

- COPPA (Children's Online Privacy Protection Act)
- CAN-SPAM act (Controlling the Assault of Non-Solicited Pornography And Marketing)
- Data Security

- Marketing Mobile Apps
- Endorsements and Testimonials
- Health Claims
- Disclosures

They also have a helpful article called, How to Make Effective Disclosures in Digital Advertising (see: http://mrse.co/copywriting-links).

Creating Terms and Conditions and a Privacy Policy for Your Site

If you're collecting any personal information from your site visitors such as email addresses (and as you learned in Chapter 1, you should be) then you'll need a policy explaining how you'll use and protect that data. Other considerations include:

- Collecting credit card information
- Surveys
- SSL Certificates
- Setting website cookies
- Sharing user information with third parties
- Google AdSense and Google Analytics
- Returns and Refunds
- Companies you invest in

- Companies that invest in you
- Site sponsors
- Parent companies

So how do you communicate all of this information? Through your site's Terms and Conditions and Privacy Policy.

One way to create this is through an attorney. Yes, they can be expensive, but if you're running a six figure business, there's a good chance you already have your own lawyer or access to one. Chalk it up to the cost of doing business.

If you don't have an attorney yet, treat your search much like you would a designer or a doctor... ask your network for referrals, find one that is a good match for your business, get feedback from other clients, and have an introductory conversation.

If you're just starting out and keeping expenses down, another way to create these documents is through an online "privacy policy generator." There are plenty of these to be found on the web, but unfortunately due to the nature of the topic, we're hesitant to recommend or endorse a specific one. Once again, ask your peers for recommendations and do your due diligence.

Lastly, while the legal side of things might not be fun, there are still ways to put the customer first and stay true to your brand.

For example, New York-based photographer and storyteller Parris Whittingham (FromParrisWithLove.com) shoots lots of weddings. And weddings can be pretty complicated. From the pressure of having the perfect day, to the tedium of dealing with venues and catering and flowers and dress fittings and then some. We won't even get into the drama of crazy cousin Lou wanting to do magic tricks and Aunt Mary listing her beloved chihuahua as her plus one.

To ease that stress, Parris makes a simple promise to his couples: he will be the easiest photographer you will ever work with, from the first point of contact, through the big day itself and delivery of the final wedding album.

This simple promise (taken seriously) has allowed his studio to charge a premium for their services. It also means he's constantly searching for ways to improve and up the ante. For example, when a bride who was also a dear friend had a contract question for his team, they realized this was a way to align with their values and decided to entirely redo the contract wording and create an agreement in plain English.

Mind you, the contract was about the same as any other photographer in the business, but that was the problem. It was filled with template "legalese" and difficult to understand. Working with his studio manager, a lawyer, and a few other trusted advisors, they crafted a new contract that is easy to understand and legally sound.

As Parris describes it, "When you deliver flawless service, backed by craftsmanship and caring about each individual you serve, the result is often remarkable. Customers are willing to pay a premium for remarkable, in contrast to businesses that rely on the line, 'Sorry, that's just how we do things.' I want every couple to feel that we created something unique and feel at ease, even when reading the contract and talking numbers. All of this helps build trust and makes for better photos, and that makes all the difference to our clients."

Takeaways

Like changing the oil in your car, doing your taxes, or flossing your teeth, having a privacy policy is a necessary evil on your website. It's the cost of doing business.

While we'd like to give you a simple A, B, C takeaway, like any legal advice there's always a gray area, so consult your attorney, do your research, and find the best solution for your business.

With the legal responsibilities out of the way, let's move to the final chapter, the Contact page.

Chapter 7: Contact

If you've done the work so far, you've let people know about you and your brand, offered products, services, and resources for their benefit, and have conveyed a level of trust.

In many cases, your website will be fully self-sufficient. Thousands of people might arrive to your online home every day, find the information they need, and even purchase your products.

But there will always be individuals who want to speak with a human, and for that you need a Contact page.

Elements of your Contact Page

Personality
The first thing a contact page should convey is your

personality. Rather than simply listing an email address and saying "write to me here," think about the *feeling* that you want your reader to experience. Are you a corporate business that exudes efficiency and professionalism? Or are you a life coach who conveys a warm partnership for working hand-in-hand?

The fastest way to convey this is through a photo. For solopreneurs, it's yet another opportunity to choose a photo different than the one you used on your About Me page or your Homepage.

Think about the elements that could convey engagement and communication. Perhaps you're sitting at your laptop, holding your mobile phone, or simply have an inviting body language that says, "Let's talk." If your company is larger, this is a great place to use a group shot of your entire team, showing that there is a group of people to welcome and support customers.

The point is this… every page of your site is an opportunity to reinforce your message. Think about your customer and the outcome that they want to feel.

Communication Style

The next element to consider on your page is the *kind*

of communication you're looking to inspire. Once again, anyone can just post an email address and say "write to me here." You're not like everyone else (you're a titan of industry).

Take this opportunity to be deliberate about the type of engagement you want to foster.

Email - If the most effective way to interact with customers is by getting to know them better, then encouraging an email exchange might be your focus. This can be helpful if your product or service is new, difficult to explain, expensive, or complicated.

For example, let's say you guide week-long, eco-friendly mountain bike tours in Costa Rica for adventurous families, for $8,000. No matter how much information you provide on your website, this is a fairly involved, expensive product. Compare that to say, just selling a *guidebook* to family-focused eco-friendly mountain bike tours in Costa Rica, for $8. Most people are going to want to have some back and forth communication to answer any questions before making their investment. Expect, welcome, and encourage that interaction.

Phone - If you sell an expensive or "high-touch" product, you might want to consider listing a phone number on your contact page. Of course, you'll want to think twice about listing your personal number publicly, lest you be besieged with phone calls at all hours of the day or night — from customer and non-customers. One option for solopreneurs is to set up a number through Google Voice, a free service with millions of users that offers features such as voicemail, call forwarding, and voice-to-text transcripts.

An example might be a solopreneur that offers six-month long, five-figure consulting services to corporations. Anyone looking to purchase such a service is going to want to make sure there's a real person at the other end of that website.

Social - What if you don't want an influx of emails and phone calls? The best way to handle that may be to drive your audience toward your social channels. You'll still want to list a way to get in touch with you via email, but the focus should be on your social channel of choice.

The first reason to do this is thinking about serving your customer through *your* preferred method of communication. If you're highly engaged on Twitter and this is the fastest and most efficient way for you to interact with your customers, literally say that: "For the fastest way to get answers to your questions, reach out to me on Twitter," and then list your Twitter handle and link.

The second reason to do this is thinking about your *customer's* preferred method of communication. If you offer simple cooking solutions for busy moms, don't overthink things and try to create a complicated, custom online forum with a separate login. Rather, simply set up a Facebook group in minutes since many of your customers are probably there on a daily basis already.

Driving to a social group like Facebook for communication can have several benefits. First, it provides a central place for you to respond to inquiries all at once without dealing with email overload. Second, it fosters interaction and engagement among your users. For those working toward a common goal such as weight loss or building a business, this can be a huge benefit. And third, as this engagement grows, you'll find that your audience will begin to help each other with their questions, lessening the load of having to attend to every question yourself.

Appointment - For some businesses, your preferred method of contact might be setting up an appointment for a phone call, Skype call, in-person meeting, or demonstration. Once again, this is usually the best method for expensive, long-term, or "high-touch" services.

For example, without a previous interaction between coach and client, very few people are going to come to your website and then sign up for six months of life coaching. Rather, the next logical step for someone on your contact page is to book an appointment so that both the coach and potential customer can get to know each other better to make sure it's a good fit on both sides.

Physical Address - While the majority of online businesses won't need (or want) to list their physical mailing address, if that's a requirement (for instance, if you offer in-person coaching at your home or office), you'll want to list your address in your contact section.

Execution and Design

When it comes to the layout of your contact page, there are two ways to go. After your quick intro and a photo near the top, you can either just list the email address that people can reach you at, or provide a form for people to fill out.

With an email address, people can reach out to you in the way that's most convenient for them, such as copying it and pasting it into their Gmail or Outlook account, sending you an email via their smartphone, or just noting it for later on. They can create whatever subject line they want, and write as little or as much as they desire. It's like writing an open-ended email to a friend.

On the other hand, many solopreneurs prefer to use pre-set form fields to add more structure to the emails they are going to get. There are dozens of form field templates available to choose from as WordPress plug-ins, or if you're using a platform such as Squarespace, they'll have their own contact form templates as options.

Here are a few basic elements in most form fields:

Name - It's great to know who is writing to you, so ask for the person's name

Email - Ask the person to enter their preferred email address

Message - This is the main free-form area where the person can type in their question

Subject line - While this can be left open-ended, one advantage of a form is to use pre-selected subject lines in order to filter the types of requests that you are receiving. For example, they might include:

- Hire me to speak
- Learn more about coaching
- Report a technical issue
- Accounts and billing issues
- Login and membership questions
- Other comments and suggestions

You can probably see how this can help organize your incoming email. If you're a one-man show, you can filter the emails to different folders… let's hope the "hire me" emails are a lot more common than the tech support issues.

If you're a larger company, there are third-party programs that allow you to automatically route emails to the appropriate person based on the subject line. For example, website issues will go right to your tech support team, while billing issues go to your operations team.

Calendar - If your contact page is primarily designed to drive phone or in-person meetings, such as "Contact me to set up a free, 15-minute consultation," do yourself a favor and sign up for an automatic online calendar program. Otherwise, you'll waste countless hours each week emailing back and forth with clients saying, "How about Wednesday at noon? No? How about Tuesday at 3? Can't do it? Great, so Friday at 9am? Wait, is that eastern time or mountain time?"

Meeting scheduler programs such as Calendly, ScheduleOnce, and Appointlet allow you to establish a set timeframe for you to accept appointments, and usually sync with your existing schedule, such as Google calendar.

From your side, you can customize it week to week, blocking out a Tuesday morning or a Thursday evening around your particular schedule. Or, you can establish an ongoing block of time that never changes. For example, you could do all your calls Monday through Friday between 8:00 and 8:30am, and 5:30 and 6:00pm.

From the client's side, they're presented with a calendar of your available times, and can choose the one that works best for them. The program handles all the conversion with time zones, reminders, and cancellations.

Social links - You'll want to list links to your social channels on your Contact page, such as Facebook, Twitter, Pinterest, YouTube, Instagram, and others. Instead of just a link, make sure to use the logo of each service to provide a more instant, visual connection with the service. There are countless rights-free designs on the web to choose from, so if anything, you'll probably spend more time choosing which "Follow us on Twitter" icon you like best than searching for one.

Additionally, many social sites allow you to embed elements of your presence using widgets. For example, Facebook lets you can grab the code for your specific page and embed it on your Contact page, which will then display your page name, number of likes, etc.

Dealing With Spam

One unfortunate drawback all online entrepreneurs deal with is spam, or unwanted email. Here are a few considerations:

Email - Let's say that your name is Michael B. Smith and you worked here at Mirasee. If your personal email is MichaelBSmith@Mirasee.com, you could list that on the site, which makes it easy for users to highlight that address and send you an email. Unfortunately, that also makes it easy for spammers (often using bots that automatically crawl the web 24x7) to grab that email to use it for their own purposes. So unless you're looking for a great deal on home mortgages, or would like a Nigerian prince as a pen pal, it might not be the best way to list your contact info.

Here are some ways around it:

1) Use a different email - You could create a new email called SmithMichaelB@Mirasee.com. While this allows you to filter emails into a different account so that your personal account isn't out there on the web, it doesn't solve the root problem.

2) Spell out your email - Some people list their address as follows: MichaelBSmith [at] mirasee [dot] com. This is usually enough to thwart many of the spambots that crawl the web looking for the standard format, but it doesn't look very elegant, and it's probably a matter of time before the spambots figure out this pattern as well.

3) Display your email as a graphic - In this method, you type out your email in the normal fashion (MichaelBSmith@Mirasee.com) in a design program such as Photoshop, then rather than displaying it as text, you save it out as a graphic. The upside is that spambots can't capture, or "scrape" your information when it's a graphic, but the downside is that it might confuse users because it looks like it's text, but they can't highlight it in order to cut and paste.

4) Use a catch-all email address - Instead of listing your name and personal email, create a new one called support@mirasee.com or info@mirasee.com, and rely on your back-end system to filter out unwanted emails.

5) Use a form - Use an email capture form as described earlier. Unfortunately, bots have also learned how to send you unwanted emails through forms, so look for options that provide some kind of "captcha" system that helps distinguish between robots and potential customers.

Delighting Your Visitors

If all this sounds pretty mundane, it doesn't have to be. No one said your Contact page has to be boring. As we mentioned earlier when talking about using a unique photo, you can use this page to have fun with your brand and foster engagement.

One way to do this is by naming your community. For example, entrepreneur Jason Zook calls his followers his "Action Army." Writer Jeff Goins calls his followers "Tribe Writers." Actress and Mirasee student Kim Coles urges people to join her "Kim-Unity." Instagram expert Sue B. Zimmerman (who uses a bee as her logo), calls her followers "Hivers" and her employees "Buzz Agents."

As always, inspiration is only a Google search away. Results for "amazing," "best," or "perfect" Contact Us pages reveal some of the following highlights:

- Instead of asking for "Name," ask "What's your mom call you?" (mostlyserious.io)
- Is your company based in Downtown Seattle and the Industrial District of Portland? Don't just say it, show it. Moz.com has photos of their team members in front of Pike Place Market and one of Portland's many bridges.
- Create a simple, cascading menu that guides a user through the items they might be contacting about,

so that it gets the email to the right place (TED.com)

Use colors. Use images. Get creative.

Takeaways

While the goal of your website is clear communication across all of your pages, people need to have a way to contact you for additional information. The key to doing so effectively is by adding personality to your page and encouraging the most efficient communication channel for both you and your visitor while thwarting potential spammers.

Chapter 8: Conclusion

A lot has changed since turn of the century titans of industry dominated their respective fields and generated global fame and wealth. With the rise of the Internet, individual solopreneurs anywhere can now serve as their own titans.

But perhaps both groups have more in common than you think. While known for their great wealth, Rockefeller and Carnegie were also viewed as pioneers in philanthropy, believing that their wealth should be used to better society.

Likewise, we've found that the modern online entrepreneur also views their business as a calling, a way to take their skills and expertise and make the world a better place.

It doesn't matter if you're teaching yoga, math, writing, or nutrition, or if you're delivering your expertise through 1-on-1 consulting, group classes, books, speeches, or online courses. Your goal is to help others.

By applying the underlying framework of putting the customer first in each of these pages, you're well on your way to making a global impact.

Now go forth and do it! Good luck.

Danny Iny and Jim Hopkinson

Website Copywriting Extras

Want a summary of key takeaways from your Kindle book and access to our companion course at a preferential price?

Free PDF Resource Guide

Get your website up and running with minimal effort – no matter what type of business you have.

- Visual examples of website best practices
- Chapter summaries and key points
- Adaptable to suit any website

Online Video Companion Course – 50% OFF coupon

Are you a visual learner? You'll love our video based companion course.

- 60+ minutes of video instruction
- Live walkthroughs of featured sites
- Entertaining and educational

Get your free guide and course coupon:
http://mrse.co/copywriting-extras

About Danny Iny

Danny Iny (@DannyIny) is the founder of Mirasee, host of the Business Reimagined podcast, best-selling author of multiple books including *Engagement from Scratch!*, *The Audience Revolution*, and *Teach and Grow Rich*, and creator of the acclaimed *Audience Business Masterclass* and *Course Builder's Laboratory* training programs, which have together graduated over 4,000 value-driven online entrepreneurs. He lives in Montreal with his wonderful wife (and business partner) Bhoomi, and their beautiful baby daughter.

Also by Danny Iny:

- *Teach and Grow Rich: The Emerging Opportunity for Global Impact, Freedom, and Wealth*
- *The Audience Revolution: The Smarter Way to Build a Business, Make a Difference, and Change the World*

- *Engagement from Scratch!: How Super-Community Builders Create a Loyal Audience and How You Can Do the Same!*

About Jim Hopkinson

Jim Hopkinson (@HopkinsonReport) is a digital media professional helping to reimagine education and training for the new economy. As Director of Courses at Mirasee, he helps entrepreneurs get the training they need to put their ideas into the world by building and scaling a profitable online business. He is also the author of *Salary Tutor*, and helps ambitious professionals negotiate higher salaries. He lives in New York City, is an avid sports fan and tech geek, and enjoys mentoring young business professionals.

Also by Jim Hopkinson:

- *Salary Tutor: Learn the Salary Negotiation Secrets No One Ever Taught You*

Acknowledgments

We'd like to thank the entire Mirasee team for their help with this project, our families for supporting us in doing this work, and our audience for inspiration.

Printed in Great Britain
by Amazon